DEDICATION

I would like to dedicate this book to my mother and my late
father. Without their influence I would not have been able to
develop my perspectives about some of the perceptions of life.
Their lessons, wisdom and love helped me through the bad times
and appreciate the good ones. Thank you and I love you both.

CONTENTS

MOM

Many parents aspire to be a child's friend

You managed to be a mother, father and best friend

Never stingy with anything

Food or money and always has an ear to lend

You speak the truth into existence no matter who it offends

Rarely has time to spend

Somehow snaps extra time into existence

Will never find another human being with your consistence

I would not be me if it were not for you

Might have turned to drugs and alcohol if you did not help me through

Working tirelessly to ensure we have what you did not

You never disappointed

I have witnessed you get burned more times than not

I was proud when I watched you get that second degree, the tears it brought

You make every challenge look like a chip shot

Always rising for the call of duty

You have made life a Disney movie

Always love to rewind the tape

You are my hero and never had to wear a cape

Evil has crept near

You told me to embrace it

Hold it near and dear

Explaining it is never ok to hold back a tear

Understand the hard times so I will appreciate the good ones

Never take anything for granted

Do not let insignificant things cause me to panic

See the beauty

Even though immorality haunts this planet

Dark thoughts stalk my mind

If I searched hard enough, I could replace the dark with the kind

You have been the voice of reason

The one who does not allow my happiness to escape

Told me things I did not want to hear, but needed to

Teaching me perspective

I have worn many pairs of shoes just to get those different views

I grew

I knew

That you

Have and will always intend for the best

A single mother with limited rest

You deserve the world

Spending time happy and not stressed

One day I will make sure you have it all

Money, a beautiful home, anything you want it will be my quest

Love is not so palpable around here

But know I love you more than I have ever expressed

The only person who can make a million of mistakes, but still be perfect

Loving you comes with one condition

And that is you get all of it unconditionally

THE MAN WHO RAISED ME

Now you have a bird's eye view of the things I am going through

You will see I have spent more time falling than I have flying

Ever since you left parts of me have been dying, I have spent countless nights crying

I remember you were always front row at my games, now you are my angel in the outfield

Raining down your blessings, leaves me guessing what's life's next curveball, when is the next time I will fall

Life is not the same

The day you left out came the rain

I do not know what has kept me sane

I am not the one to complain, but I cannot contain the strain on my brain

If I knew life could cause all of this I would have asked if it could spare me the pain

In the blink of an eye my happiness went down the drain

I wish you were here because we had so much left to do

Like the birth of your grand kids and the day I say I do

I love and miss you pops, but I am sure that is something you already knew

It has been six years and I have run out of tears

I am not sure how much time has to pass; I am not sure when the pain will fade

Maybe at some point someone will remove this blade from this broken heart

But I should have had more time with you from the very start

I wish there were a way to turn the clocks back

I will strap on our memories and carry them forever, like a backpack

And just for taking you God can kiss my ball sack

I wish I could spend one more day with you

I would do anything to see you or hear your voice

If only I was given the choice

I do not believe you are in a better place

If I had it my way you would have never left

But I guess it is time to accept you are gone

It is not a dream or a nightmare

Unfortunately, it is just a reality that I wish was a fallacy

I always hoped I was making you proud

Knowing you if I did what I loved you would be happy

Words will never do a justice, but I am so grateful to have had you as a father

I just wish I had the chance to thank you

I will take the opportunity now

Thank you for the love, laughter and advice

Until we meet again in paradise

DISTORTING MIRROR

I am staring into space

Something is looking back at me

It is triggering stimuli inside my eye

My blood pressure is rising so high

Looks are deceiving, but my image proves that is a lie

That thing starring back at me is my reflection

My face has origins from another dimension

Clothes are not fitting me properly and that has caught my attention

People see me and look shocked

The attention is difficult to absorb if only their sight had a temporary suspension

Low self-esteem enables hard feeling retention

My conscious causes nothing, but trouble I wish I could give it permanent detention

My appearance means a great deal

Working tirelessly, but I cannot bargain how I feel

Either my confidence is flying high or I am afraid to eat a meal

There is no in between, but my thoughts are on a slippery slope like walking on a banana peel

Eating right, making healthy choices

All just to be brought down by the condescending voices

You try to ignore the insults, but it only leads to injury

Physical and mental health is shattered

My opinion should be the only one that matters

Some days I am not as strong as others

Sometimes I can block out the hate

Other times I cannot block out the words someone mutters

No matter how much work I put in

No matter how hard I try

Some days that image in the mirror makes me cry

Eating right, urges against will power in this lifelong fight

That fire can be hard to ignite, but my confidence needs to take flight

Or else I will drive myself insane over insecurities

Only I am the judge and the jury

My thoughts are the executioner

Not another depressing thought will enter my head not even from lucifer

So, mirror, mirror on the wall

You no longer decide who is the fairest of them all

STANDARDS

Everyone sets the bar low, it is on the fucking ground

Might as well treat it as a jump rope because I will skip and hop
until I am over everyone to become the best around

My life is like a game of double Dutch

Once I find my rhythm no one is more clutch

My skills and work ethic are second to none, no one can touch

Quick to the trigger, I got that trigger finger

I am small, but my heart could not be bigger

Often, my life has put me through the ringer

But it is not the size of the dog it is the size of the fight in the dog

And I am a mother fucking pit with no intent to sit

Life is not a parade because I am not watching a soul walk by

I am going to be the only one a float

I will not be denied, I am on a mission

Overcoming each one of life submissions

I have dealt with a deadbeat who did not care bother

The death of my father

Injuries that kept me from my dreams

My mom raised me to realize things are not always as bad as they seem

School kicked my ass

I guess you can say I was out of my class

Days can be bad, but remember they could always be worse

Count your blessings

Do not spend a minute resting

Work, grind do what you must do to be the best thing going in your life

If you do not you will get thrown under the knife and cut out
Nothing will change if you bitch and pout

Standards?

Nowadays people make fools of themselves for clout

In route to the easy way out

Money equals happiness and those who say that are kind of right
How can we be happy when our pockets are tight?

Social media has some sore sights

These kids are standing in circles throwing up chairs

It is really like no one cares

Or fifteen-year-old walking around with a juul or a vape

While someone could be dying in the street and all anybody does is get the tape

Little kids asking me to go buy juul pods and on the side have tide pods

But these millennials are worried about climate change

You kids are not going to live long enough to see it

I blame your parents for not wanting to deal with you but if you were them would you want to?

But you guys keep that same energy someone must bag my groceries

In the meantime, I will just stack up my bread

I will be on top of the pedestal

In my throne with all of you in view

Through my lens that skewed

I do not see failure

I see the opportunity to turn lemons into iced tea

Life will not be sour only sweet to me

THE BREAKUP

It has taken me a long time to put this into words

I did not want to write this to be petty or voice my anger

This weight needs to be lifted because you were an anchor

Holding me down, depleting my emotions

On my surface I was calm and collected, but deep down it was like a storm in the ocean

Our days were wearing down

The happiness that was once there started to dwindle day by day

You used to brighten my day like a sun ray

Now you are more like a ray gun because you zapped my happiness away

No matter how tough things got I tried to never stray

At some point I could not hold on anymore

Seeing you once or twice a week felt like a chore

I remember a time when I wanted you around every second

But then seconds seemed like an eternity and every time I would leave it was urgently

The love I had for you was so sure, but then at one point there was uncertainty

I would brush it off and try not to worry

But those thoughts always returned in a hurry

The night we broke up, I called you first

I told you I needed to see you and we both knew it was for the worst

You got in my car, saw my look of despair, which triggered a scare

I looked you in the eyes and told you that I cannot do it anymore, it is over

I have never seen such sadness in my life, it was like I cut her heart out with a knife

Had it in my hands and squeezed until it broke

Then she finally spoke

With tears pouring down, asked me what happened

We spent three hours that night talking

Mostly her

I wanted us to be able to have closure, but things did not end well

She bottled so many things up, but I could never tell

I am not perfect, neither was she, but we were not meant to be

She was not goal oriented

We did not spend enough time naked

She made emotional decisions instead of logical ones which I hated

I was not open enough; communication is supposed to be sacred

I should have been more spontaneous, but I could not deal with her family's craziness

If I am with you it is because I want to be with you long term

I want to be buried together, no matter the weather I want you to be my treasure in this lifelong adventure

She got out of my car and slammed the door shut

I knew I was watching her walk away for the last time

Sadness lingered and it was not going to go away quickly, I figured

I still wanted to be a part of her life, but it was not in the cards

A week later I looked like the joker

She posted a picture in her bed with a new man

I sat back and realized this was a part of some plan

She had to be cheating, there must have been some guy she was meeting

Maybe it was her way to cope, I am not certain

But that last gesture is what finally closed the curtain

That act shined light onto the situation

For over a year I avoided flirtation

Now I feel time has run its course and I need to move on

My ex helped me realize that I have things to work on, but a lot to offer

I have no regrets; without that experience I would not be who I am today

I hope there is someone out there who wants me, I will pray

ALONE IN THE DARKNESS

I am going to be

I am going to be

I am going to be alone in the darkness

I am going to be

Alone in the darkness

These thoughts seem to haunt me

As I try to lay my head down and fall asleep

The thought of no one wanting me truly bothers me

Scrolling through social media love is all I can see

It cannot be everyone else, the problem must be me

I am the common denominator and as time goes by, I lose a fraction of me

These days I am finding it hard to give one hundred percent of me

My love will not cost a thing just reciprocate it and mine will be free

What am I supposed to do, beg and plea?

How could someone be interested if desperation is all they see?

I am going to be alone in the darkness

I am going to be

I am going to be

I am going to be alone in the darkness

I am not quite sure, but love today is not as pure as it was years ago when people did not advertise themselves as a hoe

When people captured the moment instead of forcing photos

Or when people would talk in person and not behind a screen not knowing what goes on behind the scenes

Not everything is as it seems, you can be the side piece or left on seen

When someone says nothing, they are saying something

I am the one who gets left on seen and every time it happens it is like a punch to my spleen

We are supposed to accept the love we think we deserve

Whatever that means

Everyone says be patient one day someone will sweep you off your feet and I respond not even if they have a broom in my dreams

I am going to be alone

I am going to be

I am going to be

Alone in the darkness

I am going to be alone

I do not need to be someone's everything, but just something could be anything does not have to be a wedding ring

Just a special someone who can be my queen and I can be her king

Someone who will steal a fry or a wing

But as reality sets in, that does not look like it will be happening

Why have a castle if there is no one to share it with?

Thinking about that I will need some vodka, more than a fifth

The only thing that will ease the pain is someone to love, not any plain jane

As I age these thoughts drive me insane, it is an unnecessary strain on the brain and my heart is breaking

Damage to the main vein

Every year we creep closer to the grave

The hope is to have someone live life to its fullest right by your side

I need to find my bonnie, there is no story with only Clyde he needed his ride or die

I hope something changes soon because I do not want to end up

Alone In the darkness

I do not want to be alone in the darkness

I do not want to be

I do not

Want to be alone

In the darkness

OCD

Over thinking

Mind overly active I am not even blinking

Holding onto feelings consider me a hoarder

Past the border line of obsessive-compulsive disorder

Developing habits

Not addictive, but ones that will not allow me to be predictive

Counting down the hours

Dividing those hours into minutes

Those minutes into another set of minutes

Followed by sets of seconds

Nail biting

Mentally fighting the urge that is uninviting

My cuticles appear as a chewable

Thankfully, skin is renewable

The frequent appearance of the psychological jukebox

Causes me to tap to rhymes that are not present

Fearful for public displays

No one wants to deal with the torment

Repetitive with my words and actions to the extent that causes
resentment

Trying to converse is an adventure like going through a purse

Conversations are like a journey

Leaving my brain dead, take it out on a gurney

I just did it again

It happens with my voice and even this pen

How many times did I check this lock?

It must have been ten

I dread having to sleep

Eyes are closed

Dreams usually involve me dead and I will wake up to weep

The holder of sand prevents my sleep, for my sand he keeps

Antidepressants are tough to swallow

Aversion leading to submersion as I swim in my own misery

Downhill from here and the slope is slippery

My loved ones are my team

I am calling an isolation, but my opponent is me

Guilt strikes from pushing others away

Conflicted since I want to separate from the rest

Also want to be surrounded with love but afraid to appear as a pest

But unsure of who to trust

Hypervigilance is causing my mind and body to rust

Maybe I am rough around the edges

Cannot be frowned upon since everyone loves the crust

Day by day it is a struggle

This thing called life can be hard to juggle

Hearts ends up torn just like every muscle

Each day I am keeping positive

Searching for the light at the end of the tunnel

For that one day when I will be able to complete the puzzle

Cupid's Misfire

They tell you they want you, but those feelings always change

Love is not given it is something that is earned

Every person I have encountered taught me a lesson that needed to be learned

Why should I show my true colors when the darkness shades my soul?

Emotionally I am afraid of getting burned

When people ask how I am doing I say just fine even though I spent the whole night crying

Daily, I tell myself things will be fine, but I am just lying

Compare me to the truth since we both get denied and no one can handle us

I can't even handle myself so how could I be someone to trust?

Never mind love, but have I even found lust?

My feelings have been on a shelf just look at the dust

Cracks in my heart it is ready to bust

Heart breaks put you up to the test, but for me it causes distress

Love is a mythical and chemical mess

Dopamine, oxytocin, serotonin and endorphins

They are the trigger that my brain is itching to pull

Happiness should be the result, but its sadness instead

My feelings are the bullet and they went straight through my head

Now I lie here in bed fighting off the pain with no one, but myself to blame

When I love it is with all my energy, but their reciprocation is never the same

It is like cupid firing blanks, so why bother to aim?

How I keep finding myself in these predicaments I do not know

I am realizing I do not deserve love, not even from the ones above

At the age of twenty-four it is hard to imagine the damage that has been done

The emotional and physical carnage that has been left

These so-called men have stolen my chances and should be arrested for theft

They get what they want and leave these women in pieces

I try to help them, but they turn me away

Puzzled and confused, I always end up used

I end up distancing myself mentally and emotionally just so women cannot feed off my emotions like a leech

I realize too late I should have given them a shorter leash

The more I give the more they want, but each person always has something new to teach

I will keep learning my lesson, but then expect the next to be different

I guess that really is not learning

I cannot tell if that's wishful thinking or my intelligence sinking

Maybe optimism is not my thing

Two negatives give you a positive

Maybe I need to hate everyone and everything

Life will not feel like a gun shot, maybe just a bee sting

Maybe being blessed is really being cursed

Spells have been cast and they always bring people who do not last

True love is a thing of the past

Respect

Show your woman love and respect

Ask about her day

She seems tense and stressed

What did the bitch at work say?

Let her talk while you listen

No need for remarks or suggestions

Be an ear

A shoulder for her to lean

Maybe a foot massage to compliment the queen

Wine and dine her with some homemade cuisine

Instead of impersonating a virus be her vaccine

Build her immunity to the toxins and bullshit

Strip her of that, might as well remove her spleen

Being her peace and not leave her in pieces helps to keep the positivity running through her ravine

Emotional and mental bonds should have strong adhesion

Being able to connect at the molecular level makes for special cohesion

Forces of attraction and repulsion

Matching each other's energy prevents an explosion

Pay attention to her tone of voice, body language those could indicate warning signs

I am so meticulous to a point where it is ridiculous

We should always be learning

Through stories that are told there are likes and dislikes that unfold

Be mindful of her boundaries and space

Do not chase her or you will run the risk of being replaced

It is all about pace

Relationships are not a race

Be spontaneous

Do not be afraid to reach out on a random afternoon

Ask her if she wants to order in and watch some cartoons

Maybe go for a night walk to gaze upon the stars and the moon

Not every moment will feel like a honeymoon

Relationships take effort

If you cannot put in the work, then time should not be wasted

Until your grown the thought of dating should not be debated

CHARGING

My efforts are persistent

Working silently, but relentless

The result will leave everyone breathless

I do not mind falling off the face of the earth

If it means going out to get what I am worth

Years will go by and people will wonder

What happened to Joe

Where has he been

Wondering what I am up to

I am looking down from my pedestal at you

I have chips on my shoulders, more like boulders

But not a thing to prove to anyone just myself

I am my own biggest critic who pushes himself to the limit

Breaking barriers and rules with limited tools

Like a coin it is time to flip my life over

But my moves will make more sense than homer

Even though each move will feel like a homer

It is time to shape these figures

Both physically and financially I am increasing the green

My appetite is satisfied with money and high-end cuisine

I will reel in the millions with no end in sight

Even with a 3-2 count I am not going down without a fight

Unwanted guests coming out of the woodwork, kicking their asses to the curb and it's never felt so right
Then they play the victim
Make it seem like they never did you wrong

I do not need that type of energy

I am lightning in a bottle, high voltage

Can you all see, I am leading the charge

My current flow is staticky and I am looking for any negative energy

Does not matter who gets the work I will be victorious

I will probably get it done in 40 seconds because I am notorious
Everybody wants clout so who wants the smoke?

No need for cyphs I can do this alone

I am not one to sugar coat, I am always blunt

No one gets in my way

I have got too much on the line

I am going to enjoy every day under the sun because it is my time to shine

So, this is a warning if anybody wants to test me

I will not be the only nine you will see

The first round is on me and you are as dead as can be

FALSE SUPREMACY

White supremacists only care about their benefits

Any other color is a nemesis

People running around with sheets over their head

If I ever see one that sheet will turn red because I will make sure they are dead

Not a single tear will be shed and if there is, I have got plenty of lead to be spread

Waving their confederate flags, but when this movement concludes it will be white ones instead

Those people would rather be a part of the tyranny

Committing acts that are so villainy

Only worried about themselves and that is the epitome of this society

People are quick to embrace their culture

They are as quick to pick the creators apart like a vulture

Begging for mercy after they stir up all this controversy

The ones sworn to protect seem to be the one's lacking respect and intellect

We even have fire fighters throwing bricks at car wind shields

He probably feels minorities should be in the cotton fields

No one was surprised when his identity was revealed and now your future is sealed

If he goes to jail, he better pray his asshole has a force field

Those prisoners are about to cash in like the casino

Trying to be patient, but I only become more irritated

Which causes the other person to be aggravated

Words are exchanged, feelings are rearranged

Interest is lost and at what cost?

Then the next person comes along, and you have got your fingers crossed

Be a David Frost

Do not be afraid of the dark

Get acquainted with the night because self-love is worth the fight

Working on yourself is alright maybe one day your confidence can take flight

As your soaring through the skies maybe someone will come along, and they will help you feel strong

To the point where being without them will feel so wrong

The thoughts of doubt will suddenly disappear, and your feelings will become clear

The damage that has been inflicted has every woman conflicted
They hide in their shells and nothing will not crack them open
Just the thought of this drives me nuts
At the end of the day nobody wins
Hurt is a part of life and not learning from it is a sin
What does not kill you makes you stranger so being heartbroken
should not put you in danger
Investing in someone is a wager
It is up to you if you want to take the bet
Maybe you should not give up yet
But I am in this state of mind

Where I do not know what I want
Do I want to date again?
Do I want to do this again?
Is the will power there?
Will the other person even care?
Do I want to be alone?
I need somebody who is grown
People cannot be fixed, and it is something I should have
known

My hearts becoming stone, almost like a bone because it gets
broken
All too often, from the words unspoken
I cover up my sadness by joking
Deep down I do not know if I will ever love at all
Maybe I always try to run before I can crawl
I put all my energy into that person just to not have it
reciprocated

DOING THIS AGAIN?

I am in this state of mind
Where I do not know what I want
Do I want to date again?
Do I want to do this again?
Is the will power there?
Will the other person even care?
Do I want to be alone?
I need somebody who is grown
People cannot be fixed, and it is something I should have known

Like me, my patience is wearing thin
It should not be that way when you love someone
That love must have been lust and my feelings are starting to rust
Quick to rush, a lack of trust, that's why communication is a must
Too bad that is a lost treasure
The next best thing is my bitch's booty
But she is not having it she is always moody
The state of this dating scene should be something unseen
Genuine people are few and far in between
If I had someone, I would treat them as my queen
Crown on her head, all iced out then she can show these hoes what class is all about
I wish it were that simple

Sadness stems from the fact that there's still hatred toward blacks and Latinos

We need more movies like the Gran Torino

Racial slurs hit harder than a torpedo

They will have someone receiving looks so sharp it is like they are wearing a yellow tuxedo

Rightfully so

What do you expect to happen to an attention seeking mosquito? People walk around with instilled stupidity and an enlarged ego

Nothing friendly about them they are bad for you, me and the eco

They could never be an amigo

If they are dying, I hope they are only given a placebo

We have no room on this earth for these monsters

There are enough demons to fight

Minorities must work twice as hard because they are not white

They are profiled when entering a store or before every flight

The state of this world is a sore sight

Anger has risen to the highest height

We must stand together and fight with all our might

Fake Flexing

There is not much you can do to get under my skin

But one of those things are talking shit about people at the gym

Because to me that is a sin

I am not sure how you can talk shit when you are just a has been

Acting tough with a beer belly and a hairline that receded twenty years ago

All muscle, but mentally fucking slow

Knee's as strong as a Quakers bar, but go on about how in high school you were a star

Talking about shit that happened before my existence was even a thought

How you messed up your knee and missed your shot

Now you live a dead-end life waiting to rot

Well guess what, no one gives a fuck

You spend so much time at the gym to avoid your wife

She is repulsed by you

Now she has become a run around sue, I would know I was in her rear view

Your kids probably think you are a dead beat and rightfully so when you must choose the gym or them, they take a back seat

You come home piss drunk, wife does not want to touch you

So, all you have is a women's health magazine from 08 and you are not looking at it to lose weight

Looking through you come across an ad about a mate that you can inflate but you are probably one of those cringy fuckers that would take it on a date

This is only the beginning, keep running your mouth and there will be more to come

I have been called every name in the book frail, pussy, bird chest

But my pure fucking will be what separates me from the rest

I am like rocky with the will to win since I am the biggest underdog there has ever been

No need for those muscle shirts, cover up because no one needs to see that back hair and acne

I am sitting here flexing my six pack while your drinking yours

That power belt is to hold back that gut

You are not fooling anyone you are fucking jabba the hut

Do not test me cause if you want to get to popping it will only take a hit to the gut

You look at me and think I am nothing

I am always overlooked, but I just do not give a fuck

I am not a pillow so stop sleeping on me

I should not even be slept on not even in your dreams

If I am then you can enjoy that nightmare

Better beware

You all just poked the bear and I hope you are aware

You will not be able to bare the reality of being a causality

Because your existence is a shitty reality

PAIN

Pain differs with age

A bruised knee used to feel like murder to the third degree

Now it is watching a loved one receive that guilty plea

Losing someone will have you pondering who the next will be

Arguing over nothing when we should spend our days hugging

Pushing someone away only to live with the regret which will be impossible to forget

All because you chose to neglect someone you truly respect

Sitting back as you recollect

Pain was the one thing that was true in retrospect

We question moments of jubilation because of the uncertainty of pain ending our salvation

The pain pushes you back into reality

Pain is like gravity

It is only meant to keep you down

Broken bones will heal

A broken heart can feel so unreal

The reaper's blade punctures a hole into the heart and soul

We live to lose things we have gained

I already lost my father, but thank god my mom remains

Thinking about lost friends, but the "r" was always silent

We are left here reminiscing about all the people we miss

Pictures capturing moments of bliss

Wishing we could give someone one final kiss

Or could spend one more day with them

Life is like a rose and pain is the stem

Slowly, but surely this pain makes the heart condemn

Feelings and love those are things you want to get rid of

One day our health starts to deplete

Our memories may not be something we can keep

As our time comes to cease hopefully, we have something to show for it

I pray it is not nothing, just something, anything

Because once we have lost our mind, we finally lost everything

All those moments and memories fade away

Our decay will be underway

A Message from Me to You

Now I know it may seem easy to act beyond your years

With older age comes greater responsibility and more fears

Though it might seem easy to wash them away with a few beers

Experience the pain, shed some tears

Learn from my pain and mistakes

Do not be complacent, good things do not come to people who are patient

Go out get what you desire show everyone that fire that once burned bright

Give this life your best shot because it is better to try than to not

Put the same passion into this life and you will shine like a pearl because the world can be your oyster

Do not be afraid to be different from everyone else

You need to be able to distinguish the good from the bad since your eyes are the beholder

Do not let your anger take over

The more you do so, the smaller your crowd gets as you grow older

The fancy cars and pretty girls can wait

You have a future to create, a date with destiny, but only you can do this

Do not believe in fate

Learn to crawl before you walk

Have goals to shoot for, but do not let it all be talk

Actions speak louder than words, but sometimes it is best to move in silence

Other times we must come out swinging for the fences

No matter how difficult things get no one will come to our defense

My heart is not on my sleeve, but know I have tried to spend equal time with all of you and I did a good job, I believe

I am not an easy read; I do not give signs because mentally those things are wired to be taboo

But I am someone you can come to

Whether I show it or not I love you guys and will always be here

Dad left large shoes to fill, but they are not my size

Those are shoes not meant to be filled

As a brother I will always be here to help you guys frame this thing called life

One day it will be picture perfect

In the End

I thought to myself today what is death's appeal?

When I go will my death be ideal?

Will it be peacefully or is immense pain what I will feel?

Losing my family is what I fear

One by one, the people we love disappear

Each time we lose, the sadness reappears

The thought of existing without that love makes me want to join them up above

How could I go on?

Memories create smiles

Reminiscing turns those smiles upside down

I can cry to the point where I will drown

Struggling with the will to go on

Unable to accept that life has no respawn

If I had the chance to save a loved one

I would give them my heart or bite a bullet from a shotgun

Either way I would rather die than live without them

Love is like a thorn bush

We will run through and test how much pain we can stand

Blood drips down your hand

As you stare at a loved one

With a smile so grand

Experiencing the pain to appreciate the happiness

Hold onto every moment

In the end

People fade leaving you heartbroken

Left in pieces with words unspoken

Regret consumes your every thought

Reeling from every feeling you caught

How could you not express your love?

Having the ability to bury everything while I cannot

How do you forget the unforgettable?

No matter how hard you try

Memories will haunt you with a tear in your eye

You will remember everything until the day you die

STATE OF DECAY

I am not the one to typically talk about these political topics

But I have a voice and my outlet is through this pen

The state of this world needs a breakthrough, not god or a man

Injustices everywhere, media out of control, leaders have not said a word not even a peep

A president who we are forced to keep, even though he is digging us into holes way too deep

The angel of death is waiting behind the curtains for his moment to reap

People would rather hold onto hate they did not endure; I wish racism had a cure

I do not understand the need for fighting

At the end of the day we are just trying to be able to provide

Some can, some scrape by and some are left high and dry

Leaving most contemplating what it would be like to die

Others will give up and not even try

I guess we will sit here and forget about affirmative action

Most will say it is the least we could do

But it seems like the least you can do

Lowering standards to even the playing field, what kind of results does that yield?

People who half ass every task, no one who gives a fuck

Then people want to complain about poverty, but will do nothing except stay stuck or run amuck

Pointing fingers, placing blame on privileges and maybe they have a point to an extent

But not working and selling drugs will not pay the rent

Maybe look in the mirror and then you will see why your life is hell sent

People who want to succeed should be hell bent

Those who want to prosper and excel over the rest, are always up for the test and will try every option without a second of rest

Now I will not ignore the obvious, our system is flawed

How could it not be? We live by rules made hundreds of years ago

It does not help that people are exploiting the system

Living lies, collecting stamps

Cannot afford a t bone, but has the latest iPhone

Trying to find jobs after years of school and thousands in loans

The debt we have accumulated is not something we temporarily bare it is something we own

Then our kids endure the same shit, they really are our clones

This life seems to be a vicious cycle, you could call it a cyclone
Now tell me how we are not failure prone

Changes need to be made; rules need to be broken instead of bent

Maybe try an overhaul and start all over

Oh, wait maybe I am foreshadowing since this virus has the world cowering

The world on its knees and not a word from our leaders no matter how much we plea

Simple solution, shut everything down soon enough the order might be to burn everything to the ground
That's what the government wants right?
Speaking of which, Bernie I hope I get to meet you

Because I am taking half of everything, a watch, a sleeve off your shirt, half your car and a shoe

That's how it works right?

Cannot fault me because I did not have any of it

I have nothing, not even a fuck to give

But now we are forced out of work with no pay, so tell me how the fuck are we supposed to live?

These companies still want the bills paid, but ninety nine percent of us do not have it made

Some of the more fortunate have come to the aide

We appreciate you, hopefully we can work together to help ourselves get through

Because 2020 has been nowhere near a vibe or a mood

If things get any worse, this world is screwed

CHARADES

One picture can mean a thousand words

So, what would the love of your life mean?

A never-ending movie, every scene captured by the eyes, feelings so intense they can cause you to become paralyzed

You start acting to a higher standard, but wonder who you are, is this a disguise?

Is this who I really am or a version of me that was brought out by the devil in me to see my eventual demise?

Or is this what happens when you absolutely love someone

Maybe they were the missing piece to the puzzle

Or maybe you are the wrong piece to theirs

The piece can fit, but take a step back sit down take a closer look you will find a different picture is portrayed

Now you realize the whole thing was just a charade

Leaving you trying to fathom a thought, even a word

You are speechless, life can be absurd

Waking up every day wanting to scream fuck this world

Tired of the games, we do not want to play anymore fuck being a pawn

Running out of tears after all the shit over the years you are too far gone

Now you see someone you care about; you want to make it work

But the thought that you buried deep down turned into an evil thoughts spawn

Every time you bury one a new one appears with the usual result of someone's tears that you chase down with beers

The cycle is vicious, you find yourself going through the motions not feeling a thing, how repetitious

Question everything and cannot enjoy nothing

Why can this life be so disgusting

LOVE THE WAY LOVE LIES

Sometimes in life

We must choose

Between life and death

Not always literally, more often figuratively

But sometimes when you must cut off someone you love you feel like dying

Mentally the decision takes a toll, you spend your days crying

You contemplate if you can make things work, but deep down that thought is not a reality

The amount of hurt you caused each other is unforgivable, but you are not sure how life will be livable

You know there will not come a day when you both can be civil
The love that once stood tall is now crippled

Time seems like it has been wasted

You question if that was even love that was tasted

Your world crumbling right before you, since that person was the only world you knew

Baby, I do not know what I will do

If I do not have you

A house is not a home if I cannot share it with you

Without you, these are just walls and a roof, you can compare it to my head because this temple is hollow

This is a tough pill to swallow, but I must numb this pain

I might overdose on lidocaine

Maybe drink my agony away

Bury my feelings so deep they will need a funeral

I feel like my arm is being twisted, I am so conflicted this is not humerus

I am lacking the digits to count how many times I have been wrong seems like it has been numerous

You're beautiful an easy ten, while I am barley an eight, but are you good for my mental state?

I do not like to fight, but we spend our days arguing

From morning through the night, our future is not bright, and I wish I were not right

Though your beauty is quite the sight

That beauty fades, but my smile should not

I wanted to grow old with you, when we both have fifty shades of gray counting down the days until we decay and we both fade away into the abyss

But now you are not someone I will miss

Just let me have one more kiss, then I will see myself out

It will be the last you see of me without a doubt

Hearing the truth hurts, you cannot stand to hear it, but you know you must agree in order to see that silver lining

Every setback has a comeback, so optimistically you look for the light at the end of the tunnel

Some rides are longer than others so do not swerve off the road when there is a sign of trouble

Life will try to burst your bubble and make you snap until you are ready to pop

But one bad love story should not make you want to stop

Time heals most wounds, unless it is a bullet to the brain

Express your feelings, understand your pain

By taking your life your losing everything and missing out on what you could gain

Breakups are not easy, they are hard to explain, but the more we go through the stronger we become, but never strive to be numb

That would be dumb

This is only a bump in the road, believe me there is more to come

GREATNESS FROM SMALL BEGINNINGS

I am finding it hard to get out of bed

Failing to see the point anymore

Why should I care? I am going to end up dead

That's all we do, right? Pay taxes and die?

Yeah, some life, might as well end things now and say goodbye
Why put in all this effort?

Just to be let down more than a credit score

How can I be happy when I am broken and poor?

I remember when I was in high school

Good grades, a future in sight and still an athlete on top of my game

Ever since I graduated things have not been the same

Matter of fact things changed before that

It started when my body started failing

My confidence started bailing

Four surgeries in three years

Brought me nothing but pain and tears

Add in the death of my father

Now I have fallen off and have no drive to bother

My opportunities keep on slipping away

I am trying to be positive and switch gears

But my transmission is blown

All I seem to do is stall

I am looking into the mirror at a vessel I used to own

There stands a shell, a man who is unknown

That man is a cry for help, but with an ego too large

Pride prevents him from taking charge

Fast forward a few years

I missed out on the school of my dreams and at this point everything is as bad as it seems

My grades were shit

It was not like high school when I could pull an A out of my ass

I sat at my desk wanting to drop out of every class

Could not make any friends

Surrounded by a bunch of preppy rich fucks driving around in Porsche trucks

Always ignored and underappreciated

I wish someone would get to know me

I possess the ability to make others happy, but no one wants to see

These negative thoughts keep building a wall

I tried pushing back, but life always finds a way to kick you in your ball sack

Two negatives give me another negative

I have entered this realm of complacency

Unsure of where I am going, not satisfied of what life is and severely damaged beyond repair

I would ask for answers but at this point I just do not fucking care

How can my dad look down on me and smile when I haven't even been myself in a while?

My parents cannot be happy, I am just a disappointment

All my opportunities, one by one I blew

I feel I should be six feet under, that might be my perfect view

As I lie buried in my own self-pity life comes out of the blue and reminds me of something, I already knew

Something I blatantly ignored because I could not handle my reality

Those negative thoughts were nothing but a lie because there is no one that can do what I do in this galaxy

My mirror could not bare my reflection it could not make out my faded complexion

But finally a ray of sunshine, a positive sign

Struck my life and it was time to put down the knife

A breath of fresh air can feel like new life

I feel rejuvenated after all this time I have waited

EMPTY SHELL

The flame I once had is starting to become faint

Usually when I fall, I will get back up

I need a spark to help me jump start myself back up

I have no will; I am in idle and I have got no one to turn to not even someone from the bible

This pandemic has taken its toll and it sucks because I was on such a roll

All my efforts might be in vain if I cannot stay sane

The hits and hurdles I have endured have hid emotions that should be secured

After being trapped like this they are making an escape

This is a mind fuck and I am feeling emotionally raped

I am becoming distant from reality

Drifting off into a world of nothingness

I will pick up this pen to vent with the intent to describe the pain I am into the full extent

Whether I am heard or not does not really matter this is the only outlet that I have got

At least I can get these thoughts onto a page before I rot

Maybe my death will make more sense than my life did

Things were easier living through the eyes of a kid

When is this shit going to end?

How many times can I wake up and pretend things are alright?

We are all just existing, but not really since this life is just an empty shell

I am going nuts if you could not tell

This round needs to end soon, god ring the bell

Not looking forward to getting up tomorrow and doing this all again

Looking back its easy to take things for granted

Depends what angle you look at it, but my view is slanted

I am trying to look through every scope just to find some hope, but my vision is blurry because of sadness and fury

I am blinded by the dark thoughts

My heart is in knots

The only way to ease this pain I will just load up on shots

Whether it is with jack or a Glock I do not know, but time's winding down on the clock

On a side note, thank you mom for always being my rock

Thank you for always keeping me grounded and I meant figuratively because I know how that sounded
In times like this we should be surrounded with love and affection
Unfortunately, if we care enough, we will keep our distance even though it is hard to fight the resistance

We must protect everyone's health

Even if you are not sick, you can carry the virus with stealth

Together we will get through this, just stay inside and keep your distance

No one wants half the population to be wiped out of existence

When this shit ends, we can rejoice from sound of our loved one's voice

We will wake up every day and things will be alright

Though it is hard to see, our normal lives are in sight, but it is up to us to fight and do what it takes to make things right

When I see everyone again, I might just cry

I miss you all, this whole situation has felt like a goodbye

PRIVILEGE

Appearing as special

Possessing immunity

White pigment symbolizes not a single impurity

To the eyes of the system no one rises above the white community

Never having to bare the hardships of the Tuskegee cruelty

How could a white individual understand struggle?

Consequences elude us

While minorities are forced to wear a muzzle

Every day they must hustle, but the cops are quick to scuffle

I am privileged

No suspicion while I drive a car that is a limited edition

Making an honest living and getting home is a relatable mission

My family never worries, but another might make a trip to the mortician

All because there are officers with evil intuitions

Struggle is risking your life for a country that still identifies as a confederate

A Black American works two jobs to keep his family afloat and he is looked upon as a degenerate

While a white man will receive extra financial chances

The Black Americans are not compensated equally

Capitalism has this country by the balls and only cash advances

Privilege is being fortunate to have both parents

Some kids only have their mothers because their fathers never
returned from their errands
Maybe some parents have a real good marriage, but their lives
were taken by a sheriff
I would rather my father be in bars than behind them
Others are left alone increasing the probability the system repeats
the vicious cycle
The only time Black Americans experience prosperity is by
making music or dribbling a ball like Michael
Struggle is being judged for having flea market lamps
People clustered up in projects like concentration camps
For many it is all they can afford
Acquiring a pair of cheap sneakers is a reward
Others will complain about having a brand-new accord
Being privileged is when you do not have to make decisions
based on a pigment
Forever wanting to live in a world of love and peace, but that is
only a figment
We all struggle, but some should learn to count their graces
Just think about what it would be like if white people were forced
to trade places
Life is like a marathon and we should embrace all races

BETTER THAN MY LAST

Everyone's obsession seems to be fame and fortune

The attention celebrities get should come with caution

They never receive a second of peace until they are in a coffin

At the end of the day is it worth it?

Constantly dealing with people like they are counterfeit

Can buy anything in the world, but they still end up in bed curled

Everyone wants to be handed glory

Personally, I want to have my own success story

I am finding success like they did Dory

The humble me screams fuck the money and the fame

I want to be more than just a name

Some recognition and a legacy

Never felt an ounce of jealousy

Always rooted for everyone including an enemy

Watching others succeed gives me a feeling of ecstasy

Do not get it twisted

Their success turns up my intensity

I am making moves behind the scenes

Curtains are drawn

I would rather my success stay off the screen

Out of sight, out of mind

Just myself and the grind

Fuck the hate and noise

I am acting like I am death and blind

Each day I aspire to be better than my last

Never let your future be swayed by the past

Most importantly, surround yourself with a supporting cast

Days can go by extremely fast

Remember to spend time with your loved ones and have a blast

Not bringing a single regret to my grave

While I will make sure my road is paved

Any bumps along the way I will be sure to face them by being brave

Stress free as I close my eyes and see my pops Dave

Until then this is not a date to be saved

There is a heat wave on the way

You will experience a drought waiting for my downfall

I will go down swinging like that south paw

Bruised and bleeding, but that will not stop me from the life I am leading

You

This time apart, has been slowly tearing me apart

I used to see you every day, now each moment apart has been breaking my heart

It is like life has placed a wedge between us

Heart grows colder, an axe strikes me causing nothing, but cold cuts

What stops me from jumping in my car and driving to see you?

I am not sure, but I would do anything to see you

Anything to hear your voice, feel your heartbeat against mine

Hold you so tight our souls become intertwined

I enjoy every second we spend on the phone, even when I tell you I do not like your tone

You are the last smile I want to see before I close my eyes and the first one, I want to see when they open

You make life adorning

A beautiful face, my saving grace the thought of you makes my mind a safer space

I want to wrap my arms around you while you wear that white lace

You wonder why I feel this way

Every time I look into those eyes, I melt away

The way you carry yourself, your personality has substance

I am becoming addicted, but it is not something I want to kick

It is like I am the remote your controlling, every button you push turns me on

Just a few minutes of seeing you brings me new life

Feelings of rejuvenation

I am feeling things I thought died

You have woken the loving side of me that was buried deep inside

The world has never seen this version of me

I hid it from the everyone, but I guess it was for you to seek

My feelings are strong, but your presence makes me nervous and weak

Any chance I get I would love to give you a kiss in a few places, but I will start on the cheek

I will give you the love and respect you deserve

That smile is your best curve

I will do anything to keep you happy

I am yours, one day I hope you will be mine

When it comes to you, I am in no rush, we can take our time

I will be there when you need me, faster than the drop of a dime

Like the cool breeze you make my heart sing like wind chimes

You are my sun because of you I can rise and shine

You Part II

I wrote this while I thought of you

We went from growing old, to dying alone

You have the looks, but the personality is sold separately

I wanted you desperately

How could you be an acquired taste?

When you are only a copy and paste

Now I cannot help, but feel my efforts were a waste

Those feelings surfaced

I want to bury this part of myself six feet deep

Unmotivated to show interest or an ounce of care

I will not even flirt because I have been treated like dirt

She kept playing me like I was an option

Her choice is easier now

My curtain closed I took my final bow

There will not be an encore because my heart has left the building

My conscious says wait these are feelings you cannot ignore, but how could I keep getting hurt by some whore?

She calls me when things are not going well, but not when she has a truth to tell

She is a chip on my shoulder, but I am not carrying her burden

Nice guys finish last

I do not treat women like shit

Now I relate to that fire since I cannot be tamed

I get used like some toilet paper brand that cannot even be named

I close myself off for a reason

Every time I am more open, people commit treason

Women say the right things just to keep you on their hook

There's plenty fish in the sea and women will keep fishing

Looking to catch everything, but feelings

You could call me Elmer because I get attached

With a little stress and friction, we become detached

Maybe I am like Fudd

Since I hunt things, I will never catch

Instead of bunny blood, it is your feelings

There is nothing between us

We cannot spark a match

Expectations were so high they launched through the ceiling

You want to give them the world and they just want to destroy yours

They do not realize they fucked up until they see all the closed doors

The sea they are fishing in experiences a drought

All because you would not give the right guy a chance

These are my final words so take your final glance

Once I leave there is no coming back

Have fun with those bodies in the sack

The day you crack and snap, please do not call me

No hard feelings and when I say that I mean it

Grudges are not my thing, but I remember everything

You have been removed from my life, your chance is now forfeited

I will not be seeing you, but maybe you will see me from a picture view

STATE OF DECAY II

Everyone happy now?

You got your precious check

Are all your problems gone?

Twelve Hundred dollars really has everyone aroused

The government is not doing us any favors

Do not get it twisted our downfall is what they savor

With the current state of the country why aren't we standing untied?

All this chaos and we are supposed to be delighted?

As this crisis unfolds, we just want to be stimulated, but the government thinks a check is the solution

That money is ours anyway, this is just a redistribution

On a side note, have you guys seen the drop in pollution?

Our election does not even measure up to a participation trophy

Popular votes do not count if you look closely

At least we can receive an award for being mediocre, but our government swore in the joker

Instead of white face paint, we have a leader with a spray tan and twitter constraints

I had rather let him play golf that way his words would be restrained

Our country has been tainted for years

No one can help us not even a saint

It all starts at the top since we are at the bottom getting fucked

Every minute I have spent in this country has sucked

Tell me how at the age of eighteen we can be sworn to protect

We can risk losing our lives, an arm or a leg, but get arrested for drinking out of a keg

The government taxes us out the wazoo

My ass feels sick it is sneezing achoo

Those taxes taken with evil intent as those higher ups gain all the wealth and we sit here with a few bucks

Meanwhile textbooks are outdated, and the roads still suck

So where does the money go, the government's Ku Klux plan?

Some of the wealthy have advised us to stay inside

Meanwhile they have a tennis court bedside

Maybe a pool as big as my house

Contradiction at its finest

A quick way to go viral like this virus

The government puts on a magic show

With a sleight of hand, they make important things disappear

Their tricks do not fool me

They are probably reading this now and will charge me a fee to pee

Corporations are receiving handouts

While family run businesses shutting down because they cannot receive a bailout

All this money being thrown around and we still cannot have free health insurance

The lack of insurance is the government's assurance that we do not live long and prosper

Essentially, we are not essential or special, just the country's rental

At some point we become used up and worn out like a piece of metal

Thrown away to rust because we are worthless and then we become mental

This country is a joke and not a funny one

We should be ashamed

I wonder how we are not up in flames

The anger is palpable, tension is at an all-time high

We already lost so many lives and only more will die

Morals? Those do not apply

You could do everything right, but your life still will not matter

The government will take your world and shatter it to pieces

All lives matter

Unfortunately, not

Believe it or not, at the end of the day we are all that we got

I do not know about you, but I have had enough of these fucking politicians

How the fuck can we survive when we fail to come together and revive this dying country

I roll the truth into backwoods

My words are on fire because I speak bluntly

This smoke is so deadly it will grab their esophagus tightly

If I cross paths with Trump his whole family will die from my second hand

We all hate what we see, so let's stand in unity

Bury America's brand and join hands at the eulogy

PERSPECTIVE

It is a curse and a blessing to be different

I march to the beat of my own drum

But I am not numb to where others come from

I look at life through a kaleidoscope because I can see the beauty and hope

At the same time, I magnify my lenses when there is evil that I sense

Some say my vision is blurred, but to them it has not occurred that different views are preferred

I must be fire because you just met your match so allow me to enlighten you

Every story has three sides

Two halves and a combination that makes the truth

People would rather hear lies because it helps them sooth the wisdom from my tooth

Even if you had a booth, I am not kissing your ass

I will not bypass a broken heart, which is the only way is to flush out those feelings and feel that pain

Trying to numb the pain by living in the fast lane will only have you lose everything with nothing to gain

Pick a lane, but choose wisely some parts of the road are icy

Hot tempers cannot be relieved with bengay

At the end of the day, life is full of aches and pains

Some days you want to take the world by storm

Other times your passion turns lukewarm

Lay there if you want, but the world does not sleep

I want success, but more than just a peep

Sleep has escaped my grasp for so long I sit here with bags under my eyes, but they are full of money and I am ready to cash out

My glass is half full, but I am the type to pour some in a glass that is empty

I will inspire those who are in dire need because when I eat, there are others to help feed

If you cut me off, I hope you do not bleed because I do not have an ounce of greed

Point your index at everyone, but life will only give you the middle one

Blame yourself if you come up short

If you cannot measure up to the stick you are not ready for life's ride

With every twist and turn you will have to learn what to fight for and what to let slide

How could you know you cannot do something if you have not tried?

Whoever told you are not good enough lied

Looks like it is time for you to swallow that pride

Holsters unlike time are always on your side

Shot for the stars, even if you miss at least you got off the snide

Rising Tensions

Like blood, the booze are flowing

At the restaurant, the sexual tension was growing

At first, I could not tell, but then her fork fell

Then she took her hand and grabbed my dick and that is when it clicked

Paid the bill right away, did not want to give the mood a chance to fade away

We get back to my place, things are getting hot and heavy

I open the door and she tackled me to the floor

Ripping off clothing one piece at a time, damn it feels good to be in my sexual prime

How do you like it?

You want to take this slow?

Not going to lie that was a bit of a blow

Can I tempt you with a back rub to let our urges grow?

All I can think about as I rub your body

Is damn that ass is kicking do you know karate?

She finally drops her defenses so now the love making commences

I start on top, but she wants it from behind, she is really into this bump and grind

We switch it up, now I am on the side

If she were a ride this would be more than a side swipe

It would be more like a t bone because this is more than just a tap

She told me to finish in her

Now it is time to abort it is a fucking trap

We both finish up and lie by the fire and I gaze upon the woman I desire

Close my eyes and rest peacefully

Hold up wait a minute

That was a little too slow pace

She did not even sit on my face

Let us rewind for a different outcome, maybe we could add some more rum

How would you like it?

Should I pull your hair back and tell you are no good

Or maybe you climb on top and choke me while your fucking me good

Are you the type that likes being hit?

What am I working with baby, can you do a split?

I love smacking that ass, but only if it bounces back because that is an ass that will not quit

You've been keeping up with those squats, how about some back shots?

I am trying to hit the perfect spot

We do not need to be tied down for me to tie you down

Bring out the cuffs, but we do not need to link up after this

Give me a call if you're looking for a few hours of bliss

I know this is a dick you'll miss, but both sets of those lips are something I really love to kiss

I always heard the more the merrier, so how's your sis?

Would you rather me watch from a distance?

As you fuck another bitch with some toys for assistance?

Or how about I pretend I catch you cheating, like your back this operation is blown

I love the way you moan

That will set the mood as you climax, maybe we can sell the rights and have them show it in IMAX

I do not know about you, but I love double features

We are the students as well as the teachers

Just let me know what you like so that way I can please you

Do not leave me here wondering, give me a clue

Once you are ready give me the cue

MIND GAMES

Substance in someone is a rarity

Preaching respect for other's as well as yourself with severity

No one can explain their intentions with clarity

I can text laugh out loud without even laughing

So, what makes you think I cannot text I love you when there is no love to be found

Maybe I just say certain things to keep you around

Or maybe I am tired of the games, I am tired of being played

It is time for me to pull the strings, it is not out of the ordinary for these games to be played so stop treating this like stranger things You said the grass is greener on your side

Maybe it is true, but only because its turf

Every part of you screams fake and I sense it from a mile away

Hoes are all the same

The only time they seek attention is when they are wet

Use those mind games on someone who has a weak mindset

Sex is not the only thing I seek

I am more than a body so leave me out of the count

That shit does not impress me, no matter the amount

I can make my intentions known, but the love for me is never shown

I will just continue to drag my feet, I am done trying, finding love is no easy feat

My guard is back up, twenty-four seven

I am not allowing anyone else in

I never even had you and I am hurting this much

Imagine if you were mine and I lost you

All hell would break loose

I would tell you how I feel, but what is the use?

My feeling's supply exceeds the demand

I am tired of the rejection I am not sure how much more I can withstand

Love is like quicksand

A trap you cannot see

As your sinking with no help not even a hand

You wonder what was I thinking?

LOST AND FOUND

Have you ever had feelings of confliction?

One moment you want to rule the world

The next you want to be buried in it

We only get one life

Only one chance to things right

So, stand up and fight before the appearance of the bright light

Heart racing

Restless nights I spent pacing

My subconscious haunts my existence

Aware of my circumstances

Lacking the will to enhance my situation

Maybe the problems will disappear with my reincarnation

I am a dead man staring at his grave

My younger days are the ones I crave

Back when my pops were still alive

A time when my confidence thrived

Now there is a faint pulse

My soul is bleeding out, losing circulation

The feelings I once had are locked away, on probation

Stripped of my innocence

Grew up sooner rather than later

An emotional crater

Still spreading joy to create change

Hoping one day my time will come, but for now I will be the waiter

Lacking a single regret, but the pain is hard to forget

Time is supposed to heal all wounds

Fearful my happiness has been lost never to be found

My heart may never sing again

The strings need to be tuned or else I am doomed

Negative experiences promote one to abandon all aspirations

Every minor inconvenience becomes an exaggeration

Searching for any reason to give into the darkness that is the devil

My will squandered; foot comes off the pedal

Eventually, light is shed on what seemed to be a corpse

I feel like I entered a time warp

I have been revived and I have never felt so alive

Remembering who I am and what I am about

I murdered those feelings of confliction, guilty as charged

I am a prime suspect, beyond reasonable doubt

Collapsed lungs and broken bones could not slow me down

Witnessing shattered dreams

Bouncing back my potential is at the fullest capacity

Now I am bursting at the seams

No time for rest

I prefer to make my dreams a reality

Sleep on me, but I have insomnia

I have the energy of a whole mafia

Do not hold your breath waiting for my downfall unless you want hypoxia

I will run circles around you until you have permanent nausea

Vomit on your sleeve while I have tricks up mine

Hell bent on success

Unafraid to be unaligned

All my life I was told the sky is the limit

So how am I floating in space?

My success will not disappear without a trace

I forgot how much fun prosperity and happiness were to chase

Cannot ever slow down

I must keep up the pace

Time is both finite and infinite

We have a clock and the end is imminent

Just because time ceases the rest of the world will not go to pieces

Rise above the odds

Our fate is not dictated by the gods

My empire will be built from the ground up

When I am on top there is nothing that matches that sensation

Love and support with a mix of dreams forms the foundation

Hard work and dedication pave the way

I will never surround myself with people who only have positive things to say

I want to be criticized

Tell me I am inadequate

I would rather hear that than a fable

From my perspective lies are fatal

Trust is given to the ones who will not enable

I will believe an enemy quicker than some loved one's

Enemies work endlessly to identify a flaw

When a loved one lies you wonder if they ever told the truth at all

Develop a sense of selection

Not everyone and everything is deserving of your attention

Focus on the prize

Be thankful for the lows and the highs

Always remember obstacles are blessings in disguise

GREATEST FEARS

Some hate spiders, some hate flying, and some hate the dark

The sound of a bark makes some cringe, some are afraid to binge

Going to public places can cause a sense of fright, even if our friends tell us it is going to be alright

We would rather enjoy the comforts of home, but then we are afraid to grow old and alone

We want companionship, but are afraid to pick up the phone

Even if we do, we fear that friend zone or being disowned by someone who you truly have feelings for

We try to confine in people who we believe will offer more

Those same people who told us they would be here through thick and thin

Then say poof and disappear

You sit there wondering where they have been

The constant disappointment builds and destroys you from within

Some of us lose so much that we are afraid to win

We want to be happy, but have no clue where to begin

Being successful sounds promising, but reaching new heights sometimes does not feel right

We would rather be comfortable since that is all we know

Even though mediocre is not as high as we can go

You want to stop what you are doing and pursue your dreams, but then you get cold feet because you get scared your plan is going to burst at the seams

You give up and start planning all these different schemes

All which have fortune as the theme

We dream of the big houses, being rich with fancy cars, but those things come with baggage so are you ready to carry the emotional scars?

Suddenly, everyone and their mother want to be your friend, unless you are approaching some bitter end

Even then they will not hesitate to ask if you have any money to send

You can be going through your worst day, but none of them have an ear to lend

People fear they will be used and abused

Sometimes it is hard to tell who is in your corner, usually they are just the ones who knock you into them

The person you trust most ironically become the reason you trust no one, anytime someone tries to get close you feel the need to run

One day you give up and call it quits because you can only take so many emotional hits

At the end of the day, time is ticking death has a watch

Either we sit here and wait for life to take us down a notch or kick us in the crotch

Or we dig deep and find the strength to climb these hurdles

Put our heads down and sprint to the finish with our arms raised

Anything and everything are possible, with a little hard work you will be amazed

I am fueled by overcoming the odds, I am not dependent on any of the gods

A wise man once said what does not kill you makes you stranger
So, why not embark in a little danger

PACK A PUNCH

My delightful demeanor is aging poorly

I think I would rather be a menace to society

Show case my personalities since I have a variety

I am the result of alcoholism and bravery

It is a miracle the sight of liquor does not leave me savoring

My addictions run heavy, I am that kind of breed

The rush of adrenaline is something that I need

Some consider the ways I get that rush to be trash

At the end of the day I am still a junkie

Gym rat, baseball bat, video games daily, Slim Shady and sex maybe

Without it I am psychologically in pain, I will go insane likely becoming psychotic hopped up on narcotics
Maybe take some toxy
That will eliminate the filter and give me some Moxy

Maybe I am flirting with death, but I will go down swinging until my dying breath

The only way I am leaving this earth is by suicide, which would be genocide because I have one hundred lives, I am a one-man army

Your full arsenal is as effective as a fourth of mine

You might want to upgrade that fire power, so that it packs a punch

Society is like a bunch of zombies

I am like Pettitte I am picking them off

Never seen so many people alarmed by a cough

Pick a fight with me better be ready for twelve rounds

All I must do is sneeze, and all will disperse

Wish I had a bitch that I could immerse in as she throws it in reverse

The longer this pandemic goes, my urges will only get worse

The next woman I meet there will be no need to converse

How could I eat the booty like groceries if I cannot even find any toiletry?

I am spazzing out, jumping off the walls

Women do the same with their conclusions

Their thoughts are illusions causing them to live in delusion

Always quick to assume

You can make an ass out of you, but I will not allow you to make one out of me I refuse to be the butt of the joke

Silence ensues

The crickets croaked quicker than only fan accounts

Those bank accounts do not impress me regardless of the amounts

Their bodies will dry up like the Mojave

Thirst traps do not work on the dry land

Life is not like the beach playing in that sand

I hope you guys enjoyed your one band

The government will get every nickelback

Currently they are busy licking Amazon's ball sack

Like Arnold I will be back

ITCHING

My drawers are empty

I hear the toilet flush

Jumped out of bed in a rush

Found out my stash is going down the drain

It is for my own good they said

Now I spend my days lying in bed

From sweating to the shakes

Every muscle in my body aches

The demons in me are trying to escape

I try to cry, but nothing comes out

My body has an itch that I cannot scratch

Addictions are irregularly frequent like a rash

Spent the last of my money

My nose feels like it is runny

It is just blood streaming down my face

I still miss that feeling like I was in space

Went from floating on air to driving while impaired

Under the influence because of coke

I used to think those commercials were a joke until my friend had a stroke

Ever since then life has been below par

I was not prepared for that emotional scar

Every night I drown those feelings at the bar

Whiskey and coke, I like to mix and match

I come back from the bathroom with a mustache

Life is scummy, no one loves me

Unable to come to grips with this habit

My dependency is a result of my inability to accept life's
hardships and not treat them like a disability

I need help and that is the first step

My beliefs in God I am not willing to accept

My mistakes are piling up as my time is ending

It is time to stop pretending

I can stop whenever I want

My habit is under control

Low on funds, but I can always sell my soul

Maybe ask someone to loan me a few dollars

Family is family they will help me

Hesitant to enable, but business is always conducted under the
table

If I can escape, then happiness awaits

Even if it is only temporary I do not mind because life is scary

I can repeat the cycle

My tolerance is growing stronger I cannot use this dosage much
longer

Let me double this dose and wash it down with a bottle of liquor

Here is a toast to my soon to be ghost

Sober Thoughts

Drunk words are sober thoughts, but the things I want to do to you I wish were not only thoughts

These feelings that I caught are not something that can be easily fought

They are special, unique something that cannot be bought

Materials do not impress me

I have what I want, so those things suppress me, but you are something that I do need

I am unsure how to tell or show you that, guess I am a hard read

If you look in between the lines you will see

I am just a guy who needs a chance to show you how happy you should be

Your sky is gray, the rain is lurking from feelings that are burning you up on the inside
Just take my hand,
I will help you through it because rain or shine I am someone you can always confine in

I have been wandering this earth wondering where you have been because another minute spent without you is a sin

I am not willing to make any other mistakes, so this is a risk I must take no matter what calculations I make I know this can result in heart ache

If I do not act on something this strong it would only lead to regret

You are not someone I ever want to forget

If I ever lost you, I will not just be able to get over it, I cannot reset

My time with you makes me wonder if I am awake since the only time I am that happy is in my dreams

Since tragedy is reality's theme and my life seems like a meme

I cannot promise that every moment will be perfect, there will be times when we are happy, angry or sad

But every hurdle, every obstacle will only make me grateful and glad that I have you

I would not want to wake up next to anyone else, that would be a skewed view

Each day has brought me something new and I have seen how my feelings have grew

At my age, I am avoiding the stress

So, at the end of the day I just want to lay with you and hold your breast

I just want to laugh and enjoy myself

But how can I do that when I do not have you

Just want to wrap my arms around you, close my eyes and be at peace

All the weights in the world are not enough to keep me sane

You are what keeps me sane, my separate peace

If being with you is a crime, lock me up call the police

Please baby do me the honor and cuff me up

Take some time think about it, these words are not hollow

If I cannot have you, that would be hard to swallow

I am choked up, arms are shaking

Hoping to hear the answer while my heart is racing

We miss the chances we do not take

If this is a mistake its one I want to make

Roses are red, violets are blue

Words will never describe how much I cherish you

PUKE

This goes back to my high school days

For the most part I kept to myself

After my humbling experiences I treated people with respect

Having that reciprocated is what I would expect

But I was always someone they would reject

Whether it was romantically, or platonic people ran like sonic

You live and you learn, giving love when it is not earned

Growing older some glow up like the stick and as a result act like a dick

That behavior makes me want to snap them in half real quick because I cannot stomach let alone stand pricks

Confidence and cocky are not the same I could only imagine what they would be like with money and fame

Allow me to knock you down a peg

Those looks fade, when your forty no one will want to touch you

No scratch that, I meant look at you

There are somethings people won't do even if they are paid

Even though a sex doll would be an upgrade

Since the only substance you will have is abuse whether its crack or booze that is up to you

You cannot handle this truth? Sue me

Or blow me whichever cums first

I do not want to hear you bitching and you cannot talk with your mouth full

Just do not chew, only swallow

This goes down easier than the truth

Get used to swallowing offspring, that is your fountain of youth

I am starting to understand why people hate me

I love stirring up controversy

Silence is not an option, I speak it into existence, pushing through every path of resistance

I will cause so much static until people are ready to blow

Guess that is why I am known as Voltage, welcome to the most electrifying show

Now it is about who you know, not what you know

Not that you know anything you are slow

That is why you have those connections since you have handled so many erections

I bust my ass for everything, while most of these women shake theirs

There are no standards anymore just heirs

People just inherit bad habits and stupidity, no one really cares

Women selling their body and souls just for some shares

At the end of the day, no one will invest in a chest because they want what is inside, which is the treasure

Competence, respect, honesty and humor all cause pleasure

These days I question how kids are raised

Praised for being an idiot on tic tok or sucking some cock

Popping out kids at the age of eighteen, just because he called you his queen?

Then he runs away and to this day has not been seen

I blame the parents as much as the kids because they passed on the genes

Too bad there is not a vaccine for stupidity

Maybe then the world would have some fluidity

I am not on a conquest; those days are behind me

I already feel I have fought long enough

My journey is over, I will let the "gods" takeover

If anyone needs me, I will be trapped in my house sober

Reality Check

I am getting tired of this world filled with these people

None of which give a fuck

I have something for them

A numb chuck off the jaw

Now you can look like a victim from saw and add to the list of flaws

They are causing me to lose my mind

Their existence is like poisonous venom in my veins

I do not think I am over reacting life is full of growing pains

Maybe feed half of the population a pill and wipe them from existence

Seems like the path of least resistance

People no longer will take the shirt off their back for someone else

Now they just take mine, shrug their shoulders and pretend everything is fine

Can you spare some change?

Better yet how about we be the catalyst of change

Let us rearrange the behavior that has become strange

For starters let us get rid of this texting shit

It is funny how we can communicate in seconds, but I have never felt so far away

I am finally doing something with my life and what do you know?

People come out of the woodwork after months of silence

Those fuckers are asking for violence

No one can formulate a thought not even a single word

We are nothing but a bunch of corpses with the attention span of a turd

Then there is this emphasis on race

Because of that people must live life at a different pace

Are we really living in a world where Kap does not have a job, but the jets hired Adam Gase?

Man, fuck that what a waste

Race should not be ignored

Every culture is special and should be acknowledged, but at the end of the day aren't we all just humans?

Instead we act difficult and hostile like some mutants

Cops shooting the innocent, criminals running free

I cannot help but sit back and wonder what if I were black

How would society act towards me?

Yeah, I am white and that comes with privileges

I can drive a Beemer and not have the cops be my reaper

I will always be guaranteed a seat in any class

I will get better jobs and be paid more

Do not get it twisted this is not me bragging I am just showing the unfair score

FROM A DISTANCE

It is a Friday night and this club is popping

Everyone living it up and this party is nowhere close to stopping

People coming from every direction bar hopping

A man sits there in the corner with an empty glass of henny

The bar tender cut him off after twenty

His tension rises, frustration to the max

There is one way he could relax

He takes a quick detour to the bathroom

Skipped the line, told them it is an emergency

He does a line with urgency

Walks back out looks around

He sees this bitch that is stacked super thick

Just like him, those jeans could barely keep it together

One move away from popping out her tank top

Scanning the area, he notices the two friends she is with

So, he ran over quick because they needed to be closer than shoulder width

He is behind her; she starts winding and grinding all over his dick

This is only the top of the iceberg, but he wants to give more than just the tip

He spikes her drink, cannot wait for her to take a sip

When she begins to weaken and stumble, he will hold her tight like a pistol grip

She becomes dizzy, has no clue what is wrong, so he offers her a ride home

Little does she know he is stocked up on Viagra, ready to unload a clip

Too many rounds will make you quiver, and your heartbeat will begin to snip

After this night they will never meet again

Once it is over, he will convince himself this never happened and just pretend

People get what they want in the end

Hello darkness my old friend

They get back to her place, he helps her inside, she better be ready to abide

He put one hand on her ass the other on her breast, he is going akimbo on this bimbo

Next, he rips open her top and she yells stop

She tries to push him away, but the roofies have something to say

Weaker and weaker she gets

She is barely hanging on

Just like those pants that are now gone

He stands still and gazes upon her

Like a predator hunting its prey he gets ready to pounce

The light gets dimmer, sexual urges are beyond a simmer

A blackout commences, so does his pleasure

The deed has been done

His seed has been planted in her sacred garden

When she regains consciousness, her heart will begin to harden

Especially after finding out that their offspring is getting ready to sprout

She either keeps the baby or loses it, but she can never shake these memories

As there are no reversal remedies

Her life took a turn for the worst all because of some assholes thirst

Now she wishes she were lying in a Hurst

Therefore, women are always on guard they must keep up their defenses

For guys like this who commit this treason

Women are to blame for dressing a certain way, but how should they in this kind of season?

I have no idea how women get blamed for these tragic and fatal experiences

Men plea as innocent after the incident just to live as normal citizens

The system is flawed, changes need to be made and not just a few we need a cascade

Because when things like this happen tears do not just appear, they pour

This is just one of the many reasons we are at the brink of civil war

Women have the right to life and receiving basic rights should not be a chore

There have already been so many lives effected do we really want more?

DEPRESSION

The days have grown long and have become weary

I just cannot seem to catch my stride

I have stayed up every night and cried

Always coming up short so, how can I stay on this roller coaster of a ride?

Feeling hopeless but I cannot stop living so I must abide

Spending my days in bed

Unmotivated to move a muscle, I need to show some hustle

But I cannot run from these thoughts and feelings

I never asked for this life so, what is the point of trying?

I repress these feelings but when asked about them I spend the whole time denying

Nothing is wrong, these are not tears, something got caught in my eye

I could really use some ventilation and air this shit out

But no one wants to listen even though I would be their ears without a doubt

Even if I could, I would feel guilty

I do not want to trouble anyone; I do not need anyone's pity

I would rather walk around feeling shitty

My life is one big isolation, everyone I meet is a mismatch

Constantly dodging any feelings, I might catch

Anytime people get close to me I am plotting to detach

But deep down I want to be loved

It is an addiction I cannot kick; I need it like a nicotine patch

I want to be alone

Leave me be

I do not like anyone, not even me

Happiness is the key and the door is locked

No one will open it no matter how much I kick and knock

Hatred grows as I glance at what the mirrors shows

That is why you will never find me in photos

Why can't I be normal? Lord knows

Happiness, my enthusiasm and will all have disappeared

My smile says I am fine, but deep down I am in agony

Happily, ever after is a fallacy, especially when you feel like you are the only one in this galaxy

I am losing interest in everything I think it is time to quit

I need help, but having too much pride makes it hard to admit

This illness I cannot fight it

I wish it would leave, just for a little bit

These thoughts keep me up at night

Anxiety is building I do not know if I will be alright

My mind is racing, but I am exhausted

How can I keep up this pace when this is a lifelong race?

Why can't things be the way they were

I do not know which version of me I prefer

Both have their pros, but the bar is low

I am sick of this pain; it is not normal to always feel insane

I just took a bunch of pills, to ease this pain

Beginning to feel numb, I lost feeling in my toes

My body is becoming as cold as the wind blows

I feel like I cannot breathe something is slowing my air flow

Time is moving slow, but I can feel it is almost up

There is something I want you to know

I love you, you are my numeral Uno

The time has come for me to go

ONE MORE CHANCE

It is funny

Every morning I wake up

Hoping I hear all this shit is over

That everyone can go back to living their normal lives

But every morning is a disappointment

Mentally I am not sure how much more I can take

So far, 2020 has been a mistake

My head feels like it is made of cards

One slight touch and these walls are caving in, my emotions are paper thin

It is like a war between anger and sadness

Happiness should be above all, it is like the ace in the hole since that is supposed to represent my soul

These days I cannot help, but relate to jack since I have not been able to do shit

I am lacking a queen and how could you be a king without one

The more I point out the truth, the more tempted I feel to grab a handgun

It might be better to go swim with the fishes, since humanity is losing all its sanity

Trapped inside with my thoughts, it is a never ending rerun

I miss my friends from the office, this year has handed me enough loses

Half the people are stressed about a quarantine, the other half only like to make memes

I am not sure how they take this so lightly; it is as serious as it seems

It is all fun and games until they are the one who are sick maybe they should think twice before acting like a dick

Better yet, maybe they should get sick it might change their act quick

Thousands sick or dead, but we are only worried about toilet paper that is the common thread

Makes sense since half of the world is shit

Maybe Thanos was right, half of these people should split

The virus does not worry me as much as these people do

Some of these people are selfish, they do not show regard for anyone

They have been evil even before this began

Cleaning out these stores and when others need food there is none

I hope they choke on the food they eat

These days all I do is wake up, self-destruct, sleep and repeat
Why would this be a life I want to keep?

I must wake up and tell myself that everything is fine

That is a lie

With all my strength I try not to cry

All this bad news I want to deny

I hope this is not goodbye

I am curious as to how it took me this long to go crazy

To the people who usually do nothing, I do not know how you do this daily

How could people be this lazy?

I regret nothing, but one thing is certain, nothing will be taken for granted

Dating needs to be a priority

I have been too lonely for too long and I am reminded of it by every love song

Just being able to put myself out there without commitment is not wrong

I need to meet new people, see new places just live my life

Maybe stop placing so much emphasis on finding a wife, if my lungs were not so fucked maybe I would enjoy a cyph

If this life gives me another chance, I will take its hand and enjoy a never-ending dance

I will take some risks, sometimes live on the edge, but I do not want to fall over and end up a dead beat

I would end up just like my father and that is not a cycle I am willing to complete

This world cannot end just yet, there are still goals I have not met

Give us one more chance to right the wrong and help this world once again become strong

WHAT IS THE PROBLEM?

Life is like a game of poker

You must deal with the hand that is dealt

Pretend like you have got the better hand, so you will need to bluff to get the upper hand

My face is like stone, it is a look I own

I will look you dead in the eye never sway because I am always in the zone

Compare me to the dealer because I am ready to shuffle

You cannot handle me, like your hand you will fold under pressure

I am here to flush out all the bullshit

Do me wrong you will end up floating down the river

I have ice in my veins, my presence makes people quiver

I can be so cold, but never shiver

Never be content with silver, if you are not first, you are last

Always chase the gold

Doing what it takes to make myself great

Pain can be inflicted; death can be in imminent does not matter there is no such thing as a sealed fate

I will rise to the occasion, like Mike Trout I step up to the plate

Maybe I am more like flair, I can be the dirtiest player in the game

I will be the brightest star, not only a flame

If you are not at my table, that is just a damn shame

Eat your food and prosper, but you will be left off my table's roster

I hope you succeed, my applause will not recede

Me praying for a downfall is like Mike Tyson not liking to brawl

Even with that mindset, my circle is small

Except I revolve around everyone else, I answer every call

It is never reciprocated, I should expect less

That is life I guess, I will not sit here and stress since my life is enough of a mess, I do not give a fuck who I impress, how many people are put together at twenty-four?

Most flex as if they are, those are the same people I ignore

Those who like to fake flex have an all access pass to my success tour

I am not everyone's cup of tea and I do not want to be because being a kiss ass is not quite me

If anything, these fuckers better pucker up, my come up is inevitable you will see

Doubt me if you want, but we will agree to disagree

I will set this world on fire because I am not easily contained

The hate creates a spark, but it is the doubt that ignites me

I always listen, but it is my choice if I want to hear

But all this shit people like to talk sounds like its coming from their rear

I don't want to hear these bitches speak and it makes sense why Van Gogh cut off his ear

I'm not sure why people have a problem with me, is it because I look mean or maybe I'm on a higher tier?

A resting bitch face, is better than a bitch trying to save face occupying your mental space who convinces you you're out of place while she's building a case to take half your shit while she's got bodies lined up to replace your trace

I tell you how it is, but most people make you question yourself like a quiz

I do not demand respect, but I will earn it

Never handed a thing in this life, humble is my scent

Wealth is something I have never tasted, but I see it on the horizon

Once I climb over these mountains, I will succeed with conviction

Ninety nine percent of us live with restriction, while one percent are guilty of not knowing the word eviction

Those people are raised with one view, which causes friction and makes them believe fiction

It sounds like I am envious or jealous, but the truth is there is enough room in hell for all of us

At this point I am just rambling

I am just not good at pretending

Strong feelings equal stronger actions

That is my first law

Talk shit or wrong me and I will have you drinking through a straw, maybe even have you in a scene from Saw

You only get one chance; I would be an idiot to let you get to strike three

Do not worry I am cutting this shit off

Just know I am always ready for a spin off

STATE OF DECAY III

Most of what I write makes me sound angry or bitter

Life's not this bad, so you guys probably wonder why

Allow me to explain

My expectations are too high

Common sense has calcified to the point where that part of the brain died

The population unable to comprehend what a distraction is

Stimulus checks, radiation tower's and extra-terrestrials appearing on every news platform

There is a storm brewing, but no reform stewing

Corporations have our country by the throat

Slowly we are suffocating, but capitalism is prominent

Our vote is our voice, but the electoral college is dominant

How effective is a muzzled voice?

Screaming out the words, but ignored by choice

Given a check and everyone is quick to rejoice

People are calling that check a stimmy

Corporations hit the jackpot taunting us with the shimmy

Meanwhile we must pay for health insurance

It costs an arm and a leg to fix an arm and a leg

Working hard just for my account to hatch a goose egg

Why don't we question things?

People are so dazed and confused

These masks are misused

Helpful in more ways than not

Masks will prevent the need for a ventilator

Our chances of normalizing will be greater

Covid has opened many eye lids to the population's mental defection

Stupidity seems to be the true infection

Feel free to use your head for something other than a hat's seat

The state of the world is more important than your last tweet

If it were not for our military our country would be obsolete

Ranked fifteenth in quality of life

Twenty seventh in health care

While our education scores leaves us asking for more

America is supposed to be great, but it has taken a detour

People preaching stay home

Meanwhile they are living life like a free roam

Life is not an open world

Pretending to be perfect angels' line them up like Saints Row

Socializing instead of distancing

Unable to connect the dots so it is the point they are missing

This pandemic shows no mercy

Starting riots and protests stirs controversy

Basically, white people with poor takes

These people are mistakes

The IQ on some of these people makes it seem like they still live in caves

People have a surfer's mentality

They want to catch more waves

Losing all these lives there might not be any to save

Busting my ass everyday so people like them receive checks

They are all a waste of space, fucking rejects

Chanting USA

While having the most cases

Cities have corpses filling up all available spaces

Trailers lined up; bodies pilled one on top the other

Families are not able to have funerals for their grandmothers

People only worried about the plans for this summer

Priorities at their finest

Realizing now more than ever half of this population is not the wisest

Their bulbs blew because they are not the brightest

They are the real virus

LIBERTY AND JUSTICE FOR NONE

Our nation is in pieces

Not even God can solve this puzzle

Everyone divided

We need to utilize every moment to get this movement in motion

The top priority is getting along I do not care if we need a love potion

We all bleed the same

What we fail to realize is that we are all pawns in the game

The government is queen and oppression is king

Black Americans are confide to the projects

Gentrification used as a revamp

Our flag posted everywhere including stamps

This flag is used as a blind fold

The government wants us to believe everything were told

As they plot for the chaos to unfold

Black soldiers risking their life for rights they were not able to relish

Veterans feel safer in a warzone

A setting of violence, gruesome visuals and excruciating agony
Reading that I thought it was this country naturally

What ever happened to being a melting pot?

Cultures are accepted, but the people are not

Black lives matter though history has not shown it

No one said they mattered more, but they matter period

Our country enshrined slave owners with statues

Praised for their past, but we could have done without you

They are constant reminders of hard times people had to go
through

Tear them down, throw them in lakes do what it takes

Aunt Jemima must go because she symbolizes the enslaved
stereotype

The only thing thick is the hate that runs centuries deep and there
is validation with that gripe

People will scream all lives matter

Those people are quick to bring up a statistic

They will not go ballistic over the logistics of how products are
made.

By the hands of poor children who are barely even paid

People act like minorities are a repellant, but will not blink an
eye when the KKK go on a raid

How would it feel if you were considered three fifths of a person?

Have experiments performed on you without a cure?

How much pain can one sustain before they start to dish out the pain?

Officers able to rip a father from his family with a facial expression as plain as jane

Unsure of what else needs to be explained

If one fails to see the problem, then they should look in the mirror

When doing so the solution will become more clearer

What's Wrong with Me?

For most of my life I have been predictable

People think I do the most while it is my minimal

This is not directed at someone, I do not shoot subliminally

I am tired of being the good guy, the one everyone depends on

It is time for me to embrace the sinister monster, I will be cynical

Do not mistaken me for a push over, that is a mistake that will be critical

People who are superficial really know how to get under my skin

I lack tattoos so that means I am not the right type

Smoking is not for me, people cannot digest that thought, it went down the wrong pipe

I am not that hood rat that bitches my age want to get with, but has anyone been happy with a deadbeat?

Sounds like a myth

My life is not in pieces and women only like puzzles

Dad bodies seem to be the trend, not so much a man with muscles

I should have trust issues, be overbearing and never care or share a feeling

Maybe cheat on my girl with every bitch I meet

You cannot eat a meal without a few sides

That is like six red flags having all these rides, but women still do not leave your side

To be attractive I need to be broken

No job, money or a bed frame not even an arcade token

Some of you cannot fathom this, you are not woken

Most of you are on autopilot, your conscious is defective, which explains why your choices are not selective

That is reflective of the mediocre life that is lived and that should put things in perspective

If it were me, I would be more protective of my affection and cautious of who gets my attention

Thinking people will act or think like me is a flaw, it only causes hypertension

Blood boils, emotions in disarray you want to push people away, but still want them to stay

It is a mental game no one wants to play, but at the end of the day what options do you have to weigh?

All because of being too picky or poor choices are made

You try to disregard the voices in your head

The battle between good and evil, your heart does back flips like Knievel

This could have been avoided if you just came to your senses, understood the consequences for having poor judgement

Instead be with someone like me, who gives you one hundred percent and will always make sure your content

Someone who you can confine in, an outlet for you to vent

I can be your shoulder to lean on

You can even use my sleeve to wipe those tears until the sadness disappears

Call me anytime, I will always lend my ears

I will help you through your greatest fears

I can be the calm that prevents the storm, show you that being respected is the norm

When the time is right, I will show you love's truest form

ABANDONED

My rays cast sunshine

But they are misleading so do not mind

Do not get close, if you cannot handle the heat

It is all fun and games until someone gets burned

Everyone wants to get to know me now, oh how the tides have turned

For years I was left in the dark like a broken-down dog

But the anger got my heart to start and changed my cry into a bark

My confidence grew as I turned into Clark because now, I am super...man

I used to be the one to brag, but old habits die hard

Now I chose not to show my cards

The years of disrespect have caught up to me

I do not like to hold grudges, but now there is so much I see

For so long I was held back from what I could be

Now I am on tour, it is a success spree

I look calm on the surface

But the deeper you go the less you will know

So, do not test the waters

The depths are too deep for you to comprehend

Once you are in there is no lifeguard to send

I know doing dumb shit is a trend

So, how about you count me out until the end

People dread the hate, but I thrive off it

Growing up I was not liked

Maybe it was because I was cocky

Maybe I was already too grown or the fact that the only thing I cared about was success on a throne

No one wanted to listen to my words

I was too woken

Or maybe it was because I said the words people left unspoken

People avoid the truth, but love to be fed lies

To them I say my goodbyes

Kids always left me out because I was different

I was treated like an outcast

Now I can outlast anybody from my past no matter the forecast

The sky is dark, thunder booms as my anger looms

Lightning strikes upon those who have rejected me

It will strike in the same place once, twice as many times as it takes for someone to pay the price

Revenge has become my only vice

I always marched to the beat of my own drum because I've always been a leader

Leadership is something you are born with not something that is bought

Over the years I realized I was different and embraced it

Looking back, I see that their ceiling was my floor

To stoop to their level, I would have to walk through the basement door

The sky is their limit, but I am shooting for the stars

The damage they did left scars, but they made me better than they are

The days of me being a loner are over

I am grateful for the people who took the gamble

And now spend most of their time hearing me ramble

I love you all and appreciate you

Even after I am gone you will all still be my crew

Until then, we got some more things to go through

WHAT TO EXPECT

I have been lied to, cheated on, strung along and told I do not belong, but the list goes on its long

Some people you expect this behavior from, but it is the one is you give all your trust to

The one is you expect to be a savior in your darkest moments

People you trust the most will turn heel and become your greatest opponents

They turn your deepest secrets into ammunition, even throw in some fiction

Everyone seems to be a roll of the dice since they have so many faces

Maybe it is more like playing roulette with a loaded pistol, except the bullets are missiles

Heat seeking trackers activated, since they are ready for my explosion, but I just pent up the anger that leads to my erosion

Why does everyone like to cause commotion?

I am fighting emotions from every direction, it is a tug of war

When this door closes, I hope another does not open because I cannot take this shit anymore

My conscious tells me not to isolate, let go of the hate before it is too late

To be the bigger person, you must let it go before things worsen

Even if it means digging your face into a pillow while screaming and cursing

Making promises without evening meaning them is like working without an income, but I will never volunteer to love someone who will disappear no matter how sincere they appear

People apologize and get my hopes up, but like the rain you know they will let up and revert to their old ways

I feel like I am in a maze, I have no direction

I have lost connection with love and affection

It is like my soul has an infection, negative thoughts invading my mind I am losing all hope in man kind

I investigate the mirror, but the visual is clouded I wish things were clearer

All the hate and anger has made me bitter, assault on the mind, but feels so real like 3-D

I am far sighted because I see the potential instead of what lies before me

The things I expect from people I should forget because I do not know how many more times I can be let down without getting upset

This emotional roller coaster has my moods fluctuating from high to low

My potential energy plummeting into a blackhole

Told that I am loved by some dumb hoe

Beauty and manipulation are a deadly combo

These fuckers will play with my head like it is a fucking dildo

People will tell you that they will change, but we all know how that goes

Given no choice I developed a switch

I can be warm and inviting, but flip me off and I will burn you like a Molotov

What do you expect when everyone acts so suspect?

Everyone has so much bullshit to detect

You can give chance after chance, just to have a bad romance

At the end of the day you have a soul to protect

Just remember no one's perfect, so do not let the evil affect your ability to connect

Part of living is dying, that goes both mentally and physically so the least we can do is to keep trying and make this life a valuable one

There's no room for regrets, not even one

WAR

My conscious enjoys playing games

Thoughts go back and forth like a game of pong

I am not sure which are right or wrong

Indecisiveness leaves me restless all night long

Constantly hearing these voices that I cannot ignore

They need to leave me alone before I jump off the top floor

Life is all about decisions

Heart and mind always causing collisions

Those two are always at war

Almost like a wrestling match

My mind has my heart in a master lock

You can try to open the lock, but you will receive a combination of punches

I struggle with knowing who to let in

Either I trust too easily or not at all

Some only want in to watch me fall

When I need them, they ignore their phone when I call

Feelings of doubt and mistrust take the driver's seat

Together they will drive me toward loneliness so a bullet and I can meet

I should not be as skeptical, but not everyone has intentions that are perceptible

When someone needs a hand, I act like I have tentacles

I feel below par without the putter

These thoughts are extremely repetitive it feels like a stutter

Constantly spreading myself thin like butter

My soul is burnt-out, and happiness cannot get in because I am breaking down within

Thoughts of giving in

My heart knowing that is a sin

Life is like a roller coaster with no seat belt and I am waiting for the spin

Launching me so fast the wind pushes back flaps of skin

Smack down into the pavement hoping that would end the war

But I am still hearing voices I cannot ignore

I cannot deal with this shit anymore

What I Lacked

I grew up early

Acted years ahead of my time

I avoided alcohol my entire life

Never had interest or the urge to partake in making the same mistake as my blood line

I did not want their problems to become mine

The apple does not fall far from the tree

Why keep planting a bad seed?

Part of me feels that kids grow up too fast

Looking back, I have a hard time remembering when the good times occurred in the past

Maybe how many memories I was not able to create that could have been a blast

The few friends I had I would not trade for anything they were a supportive cast

Regrets are not something I possess, but I could have stressed less

Life cannot be lived perfectly

There's always room for a little mess

It was not until the age of twenty-three that I indulged with booze

Accompanied by my closest friends; how could I refuse?

After a few sips, my hands tingled, slow motion occurred

The best part was my happiness and that is the part I am addicted to

Being surrounded by your loved one's while altering your mental state

One day when you tell the stories wanting to recreate a crazy night or a certain date

I am addicted to the laughter and the joy, above all the feeling of being wanted

Being a part of something greater than yourself

Sharing your life with people who want you around

For years I lacked this aspect

Subconsciously, I longed to connect and earn love and respect

Now that I have it, I will not ever let go

This is an addiction I will not kick

I want to thank the people who support and care about me

If it were not for them, I am not sure where I would be

Cannot wait to see you all and share a twisted tea

EVERLASTING MOMENTS

If you asked me a few years ago
The chances of me drinking alcohol was zero
Everyone follows up with, "Why Joe?"
Allow me to explain
My family is insane
Addiction runs so deep into their main veins
Circulating until it cuts off the brain and everyone else receives
pain
Many have been pushed away
Relationships are unable to be sustained

All that I have seen
All that I have heard
I was always afraid of what I would do when my words were
slurred
The thought of losing everyone over some drinks is absurd
People use alcohol to escape and I call them cowherds
My younger self preferred a night filled with thoughts not
blurred
I have an addictive personality
My addiction levitates towards the things that are healthy
Exercise, proper foods choices and supportive voices

At the age of twenty-three I would drink and be guilt free
I never thought that would be me because I never thought how
fun it could be
My fear and conscious collides
With my friends by my side a part of me no longer hides
I took the chance
Reminiscing of that day, I only have genuine things to say
I am happy things worked out this way

Now the world sees me as I am twisted
All thanks to some loving friends who assisted with this step

I will not ever say I crave that taste
Never will I understand how people used it when they have time
to waste
Drinking creates everlasting moments
Memories so fond you take them to the grave and beyond
That is what I am addicted to
Knowing that these are the best times and never wanting to leave
them
You try to recreate those exact moments
That lightning in the bottle
All those times I tried to walk, but would wobble
The never ending smiles and laughs
Bonding so close we all walk life on the same path
Those are people who help you create everlasting moments

WHITE AMERICA

The flag by which we stand

Has been befouled in each part of our land

Our allegiance low in demand

Divisible down to our last strand

No liberty

Just a surplus of injustice

This corruption has caused significant destruction for all

Stars and stripes

Prejudices and gripes

Sexism, racism and profiling

Hate comes in different types

Those sworn to protect have become the prime suspect

Police brutality is not a fallacy

Attempts to deny this truth, but a difficult task with each casualty

Innocent lives taken

Ignorance denies the ability for the privilege to awaken

Heart breaking stories on the news

Articles of people who were nonguilty, defenseless and harmless

Murdered for looks of suspicion

Excessive force, cutting oxygen off past the point of submission

Forcing an armless man to exit the vehicle

Then open fire that leaves him well past critical

Anger directed towards the wrong knee

Their mentality is "Well it wasn't me"

The entitlement and immunity prevent a sense of unity in our communities

Struggling to comprehend how people are judged by the pigment of their skin

Speaking of which

Rest in peace to Arbury, Floyd and Martin

Prayers go out to their families during this emotional tailspin

We can give our condolences and sympathy

Change is needed and only time has shown that will not happen instantly

People preach all lives matter

How can this be true when it is the blood of black citizens that is splattered?

The time for peaceful protests has concluded

It is time to fight back and everyone needs to be included

Together we must stand against the system because we are at our weakest when secluded

Let us be the catalyst of change so that one day the hate and hardships will be eluded

Generations of damage to undo

The hate is taught to each child anew

Our focus should be on the youth

The older generations are a lost cause to tell you the truth

The children of today need to learn to love and accept all

The domino effect states once one falls, they all start to fall

Once that happens love will rise above all

MOVING ON

With you I had a full life

Every day I woke up fully charged

But you cannot be my plug anymore maybe it is time for a new outlet

Our circuit is broken, there is no happiness just a direct path to misery

Just like that, we blew up our history and our love seems like a mystery

I took the liberty of moving on, but it is not a victory because I will never find that synergy with anybody

Even though things were rocky

We always rolled with the punches

Now it is time to pack up my things like lunches

Except this is hard to swallow

As I sit here my heart feels hollow

Rooms filled with memories, but now it is the place I sit and wallow

In my own sorrow

Does anyone have any happiness I can borrow?

Right now, I feel like there is no tomorrow

I am a mess in distress, and I want to go somewhere no one can follow

Maybe Greece to seek healing from the God Apollo

Staring at my phone fighting the urge

Those pictures and your number need to go, my phone needs the cleansing it is time to purge

I must suppress these feelings, so in the water they will submerge

All for a new man to emerge

No regrets

I am thankful for every lesson

Every curse is a blessing

We meet everyone for a reason

I thought our souls connected for more than just pleasing

Turns out you were just a demon

Looks will always be deceiving

In the end, I am the one who ends up grieving

Do I Believe?

If you struggle with confidence, then nod in agreement

Some days I feel my best is decent

My latest accomplishment has not been recent

Dwelling with thoughts that are negative and frequent

I went from hell bent to questioning how my time was spent

My confidence went from a top five rank to unseeded

Vulnerable and insecure with a smile that has receded

Flipped and turned upside down

Sadness can cause death if left untreated

Moods are infectious

I need a happiness injection double, triple the dose so I can chase this ghost called perfection

Searching for the roots of my problem

It is time to embrace rejection

That is why my confidence has a weak signal

Finally, I made the connection

I used to be self-centered, always wanted the attention

Maybe it is time to be conceited

Father time has not been defeated

People claim they can beat it

In one hundred years my claim will be completed

In the meantime, I will continue to eat and

History will not be repeated

So, hold your applause and remain seated

I have been bruised, but never beaten

Passion and will are the only things needed

No one can stop me not even if they cheated

Haters tell me I cannot

I will sit there and repeat it

Utilize every ounce of anger until all my energy is depleted

Words of hurt or comfort will not go unheeded

Comfort feels pleasing, but my best comes when I am heated

My work will not cease until those gates open and I am greeted

By this so-called God

This will be my most important meeting

Hopefully, he has open seating

THE LAST STRAW

They say save your best for last

I have told many stories about my life and its cast

My best writing has been a result of anger

The bitterness ends here with this tale

About a poor excuse of a male

It must be sad when your own mother does not want you around

I do not blame her; I would rather see you six feet in the ground

Why are you still here?

Do you even have a purpose?

You will probably think about that and end up wordless because you are worthless

All your dirty laundry is coming to the surface

Nervous? You should be

This will be a punch to your cervix

Remember how the cops were called on you multiple times for everyone to see?

Could not be me

How about when you ended up in anger management because of that guilty plea?

Could not be me

Pushed away every single part of your family?

Could not be me

Moved out to Jersey and no one could see me

Put my life at risk because of some long island iced teas

Unfortunately, the only person who suffered was me

Treated your sister like dirt, now she lies in it

Rest in Peace Aunt Jo, wish we could have connect all those years ago

Bridges burnt; tables turned not an ounce of love left to be earned Third times a charm?

Funny because you have two ex-wives and one pending maybe it's time to sound the alarm

Your pockets are empty you might have to give them an arm

All these divorces do you even have half of anything to give?

Maybe half of your mother's futon

That ego has become so brittle it is as fragile as a crouton

All these words and thoughts are me crushing it with my combat boots on

Your fifty-five years old do not you think it is time to move on?

Broken down old man with no plan

Days spent self-loathing and eroding

While I sit here hoping to hear about your heart exploding

You did not teach me much, but taught me how to not treat people

The mistakes that you made turned your life into shit

Regret is the main source of your pain

After all these years all you can do is flush life down the drain

Do not ever use Dave's name in vain

You say things for attention

Desperation is your natural complexion

You used your words to belittle people

Attempted to shut them down

Watching yourself be replaced gave you the biggest frown

Dave was a king

He was given the love and a crown

You are nothing, but a broken-down clown

From a young age I watched you verbally and physically abuse your fiancé`

Drive me around intoxicated on a rainy day

You told me you have better things to do when I had baseball to play

Missed both of my graduations with poor excuses

That is what alcoholics and drug addicts do when they pile up the uses

Your father was never around, and you vowed to be different

You were, just worse than him

I would rather not have someone around than to have them constantly hurt myself and loved ones

After all this time what do you have to show?

I would say me, but I am just a waste of semen

But when I look at you, I do not see a father or man

Just an overweight, selfish, shallow, bitter and battered child

A child who has unresolved issues, but fuck that you are not getting any tissues

Karma finally poked its head and bites you

Its jaw locked so tight

For all the times you did wrong instead of right

Therefore, I must write

To rid myself of all this anger

I can no longer live my life this bitter

Your like a splinter

This consistent sharp pain in my brain

I need to remove you

It is time for me to heal because I have no time left for you to steal

I have been stuck in this dark place mentally and I am breaking out

Now you are dead to me without a doubt

Biography

This book was not fabricated intentionally. Writing is a means of coping for me but realizing that my words told stories. The intention was to discuss things I have struggled with while. Additionally, I touched upon current world issues and hardships an individual may endure in their lifetime. My pieces portray sadness and anger but included some hope and motivation because life can always be worse. I was hesitant to put my work out to the public, but I hope that the reader enjoys and maybe will be able to see things through a new perspective or will be able to relate.